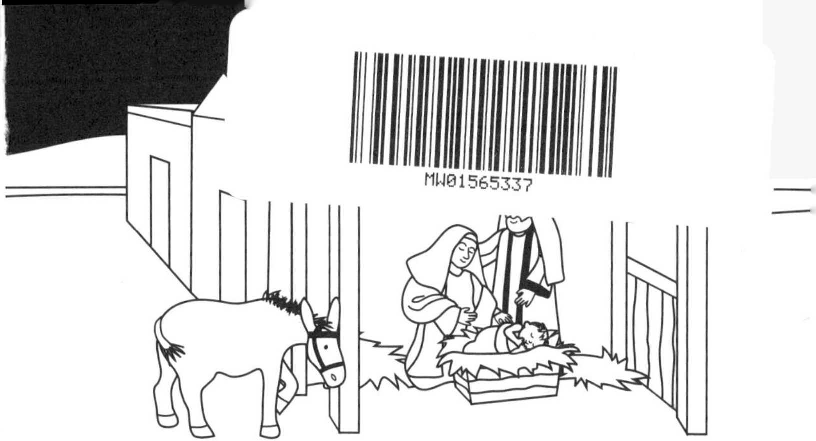

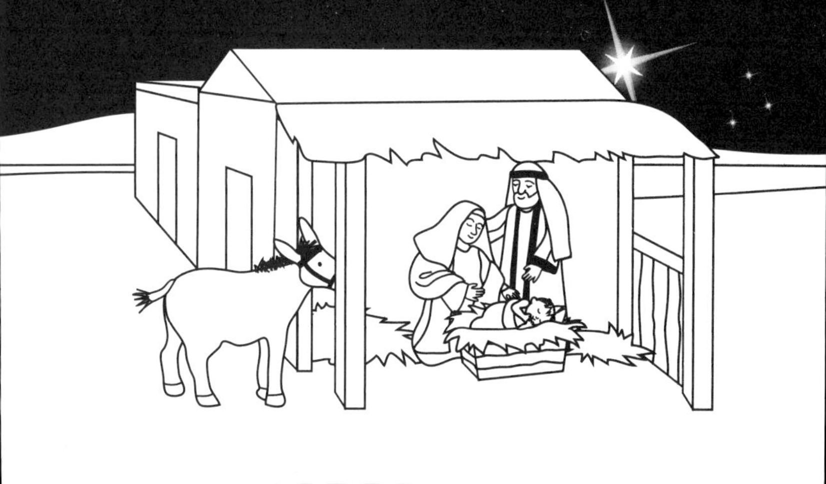

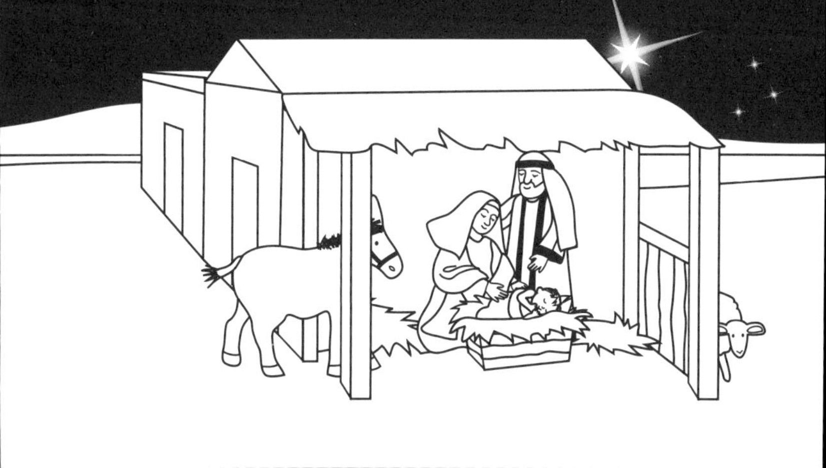

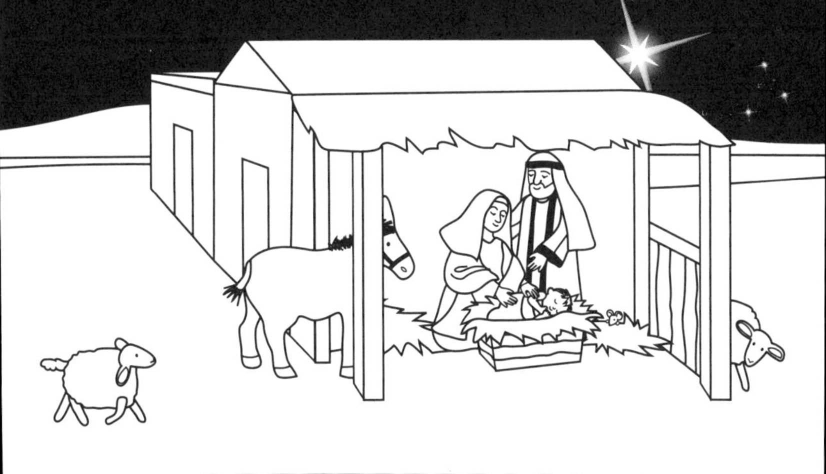

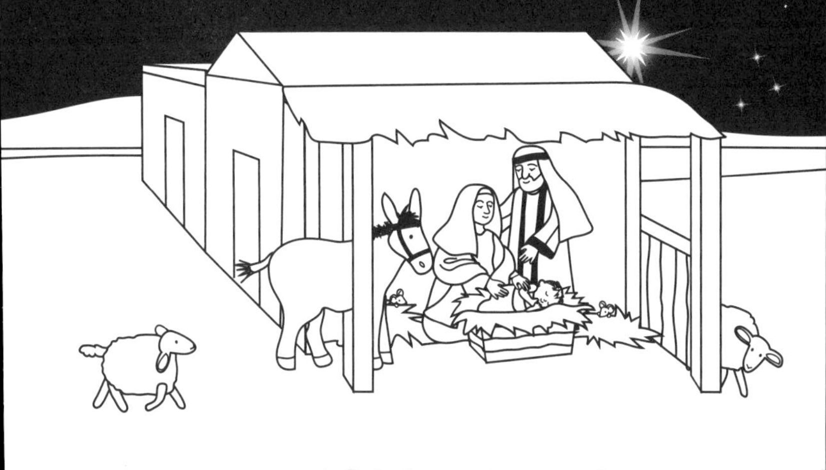

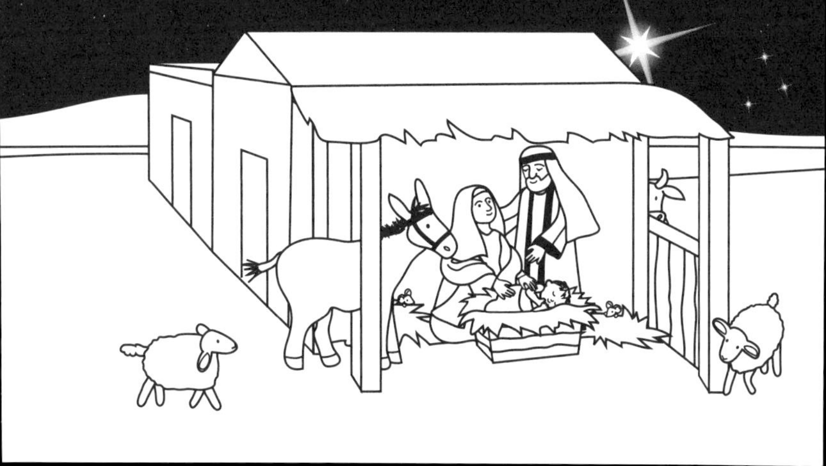

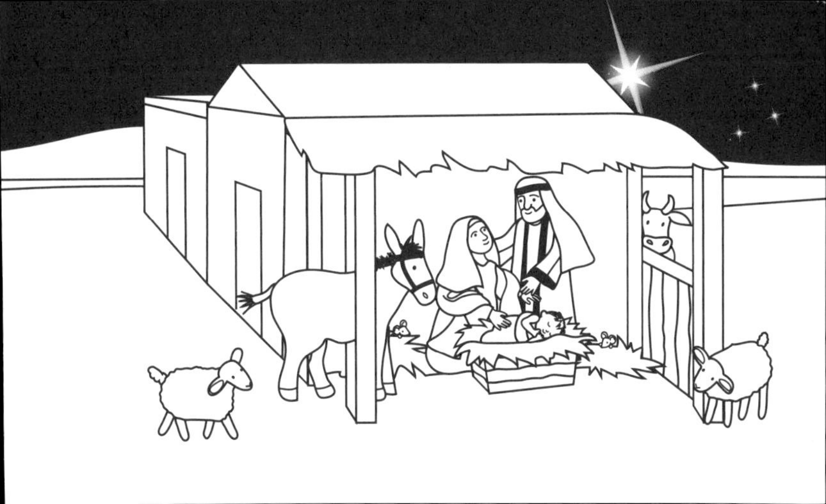

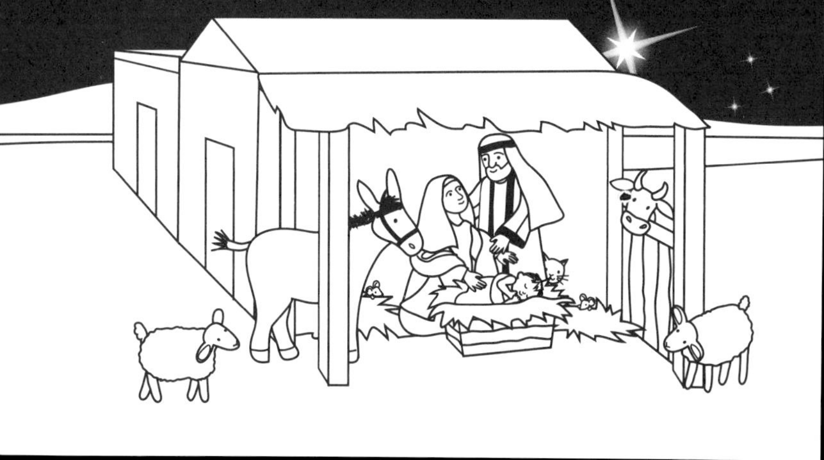

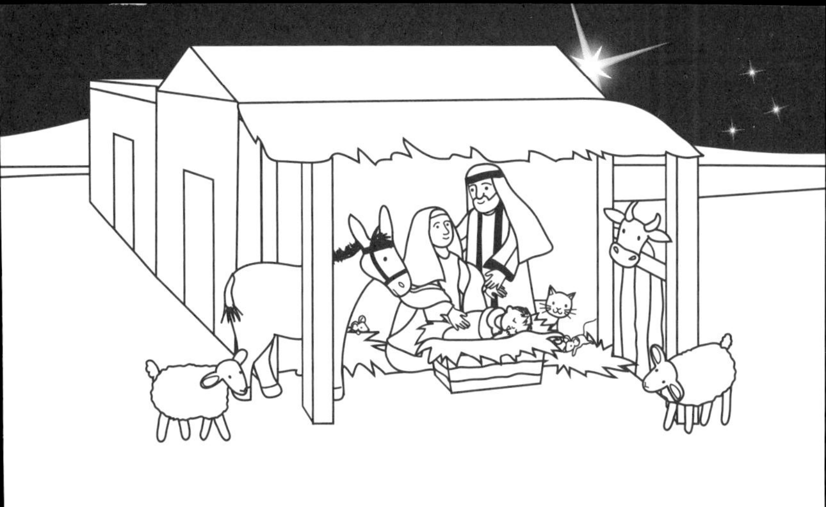

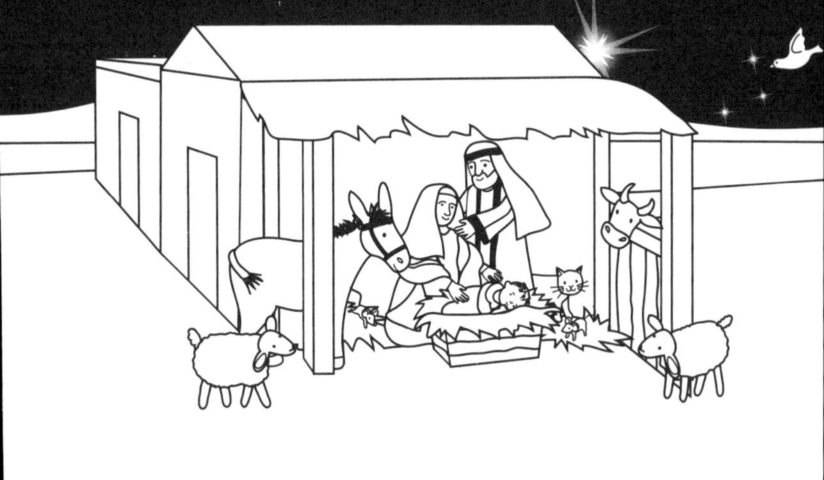

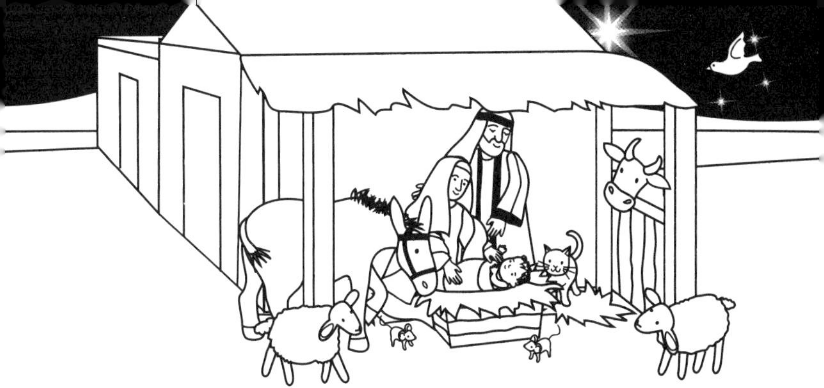

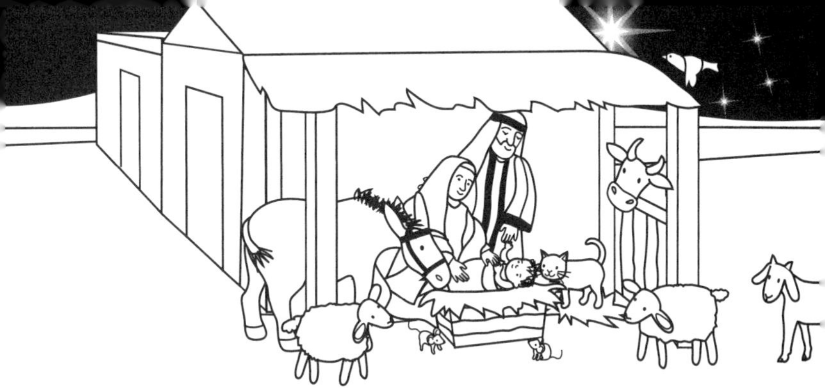

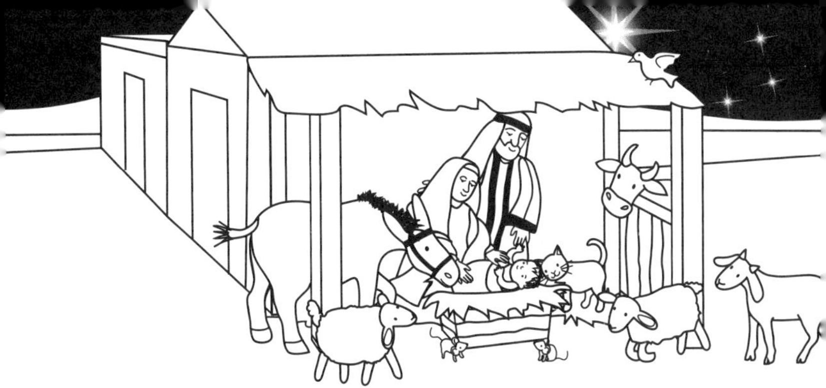

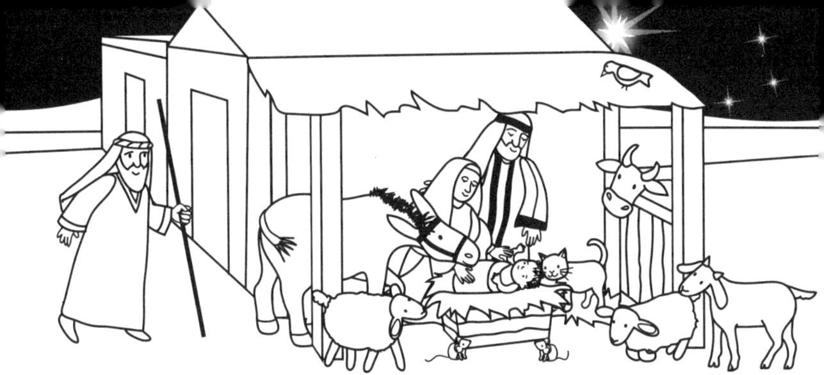

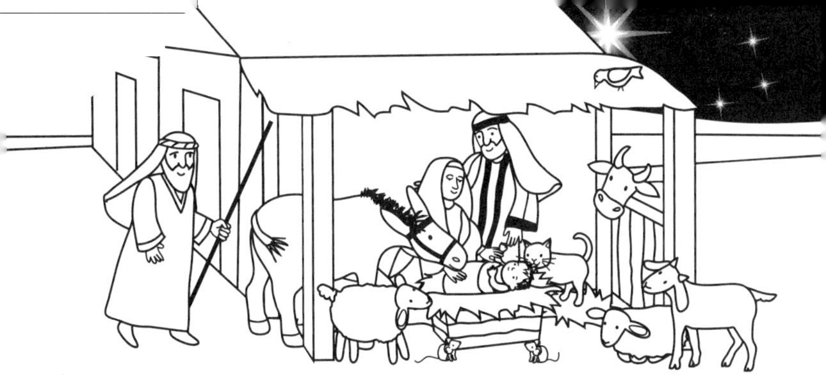

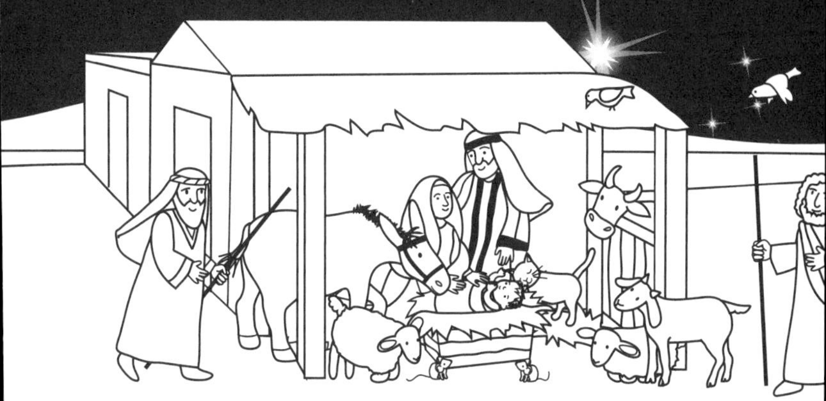

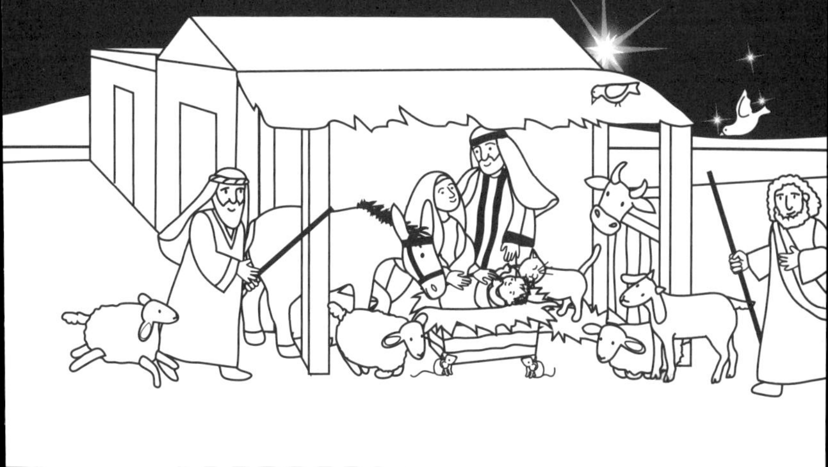

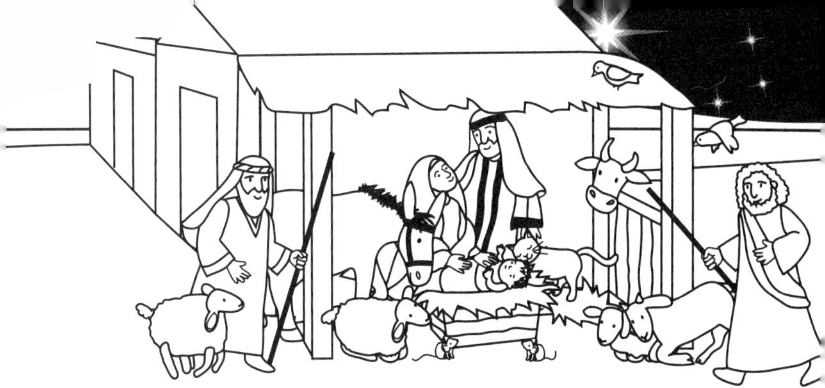

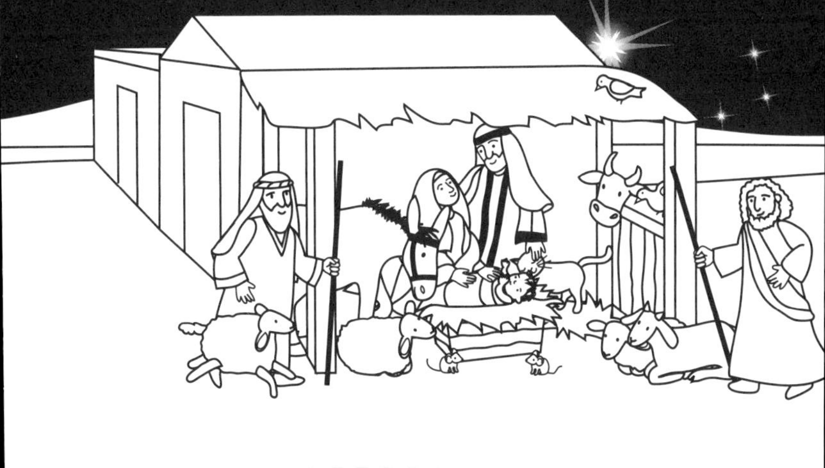

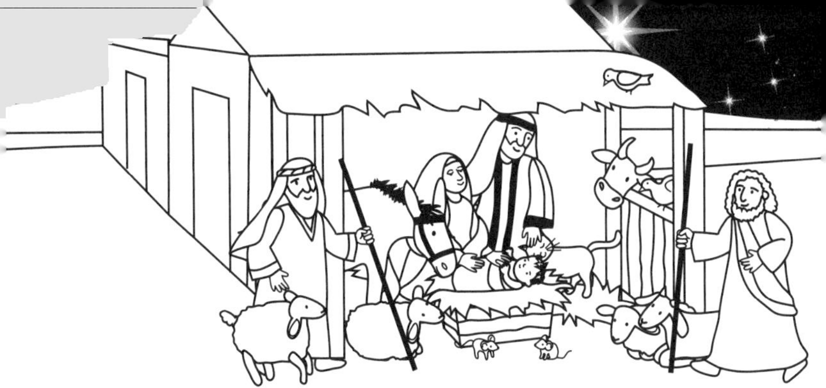

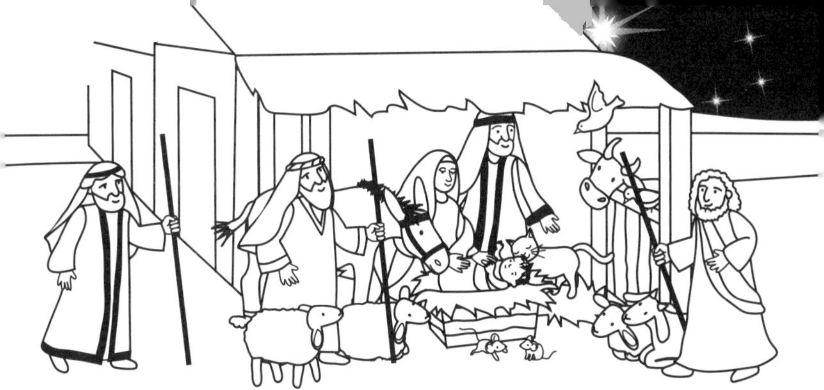

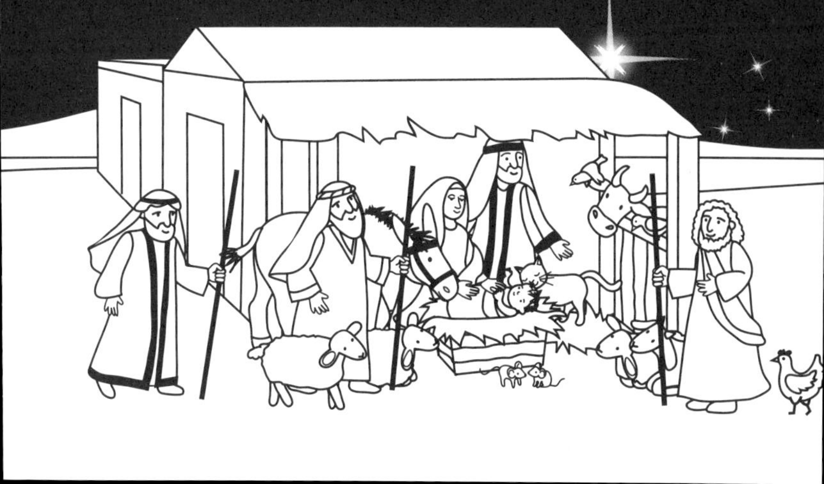

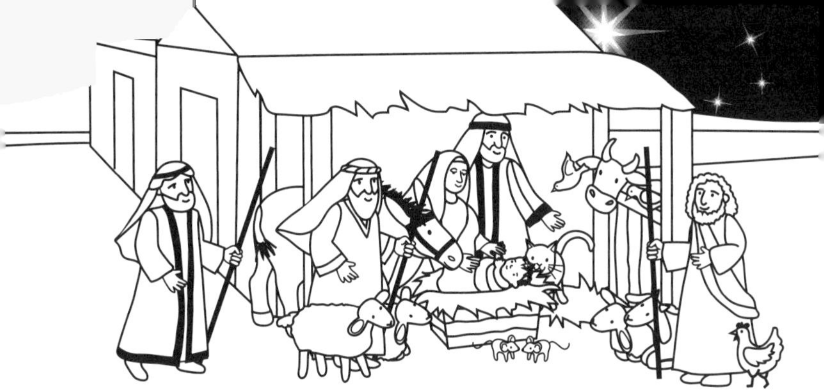

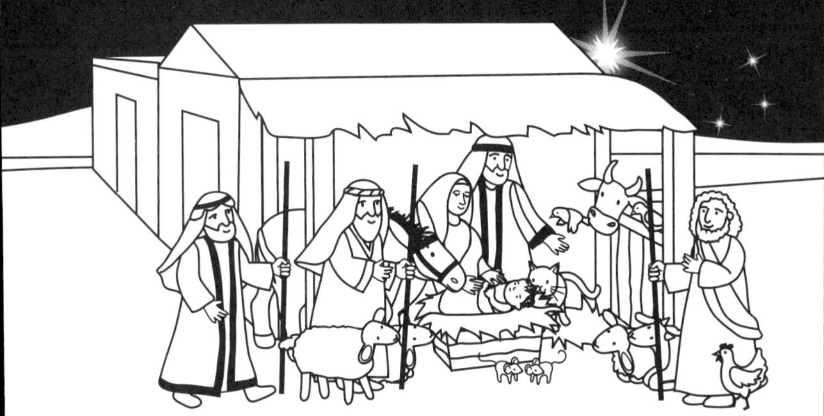

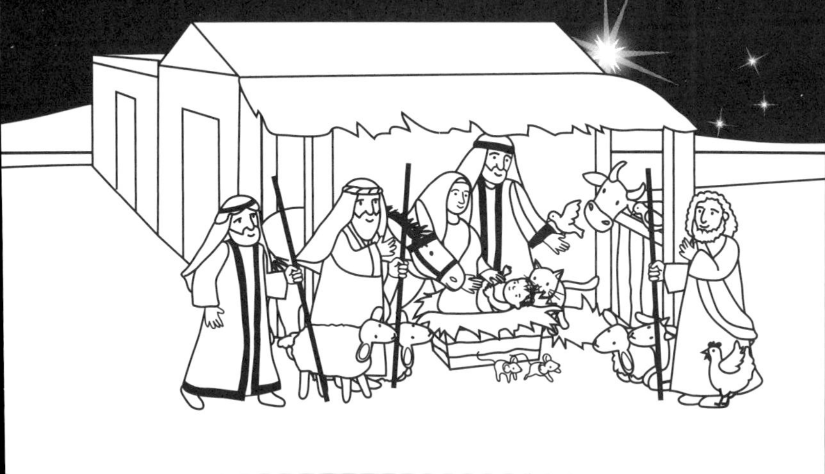

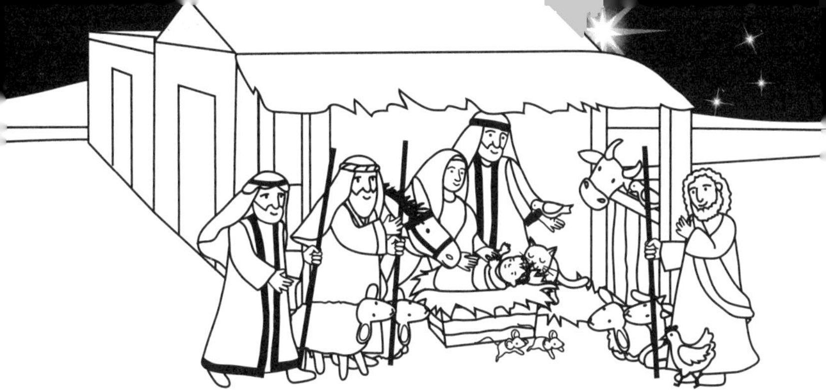

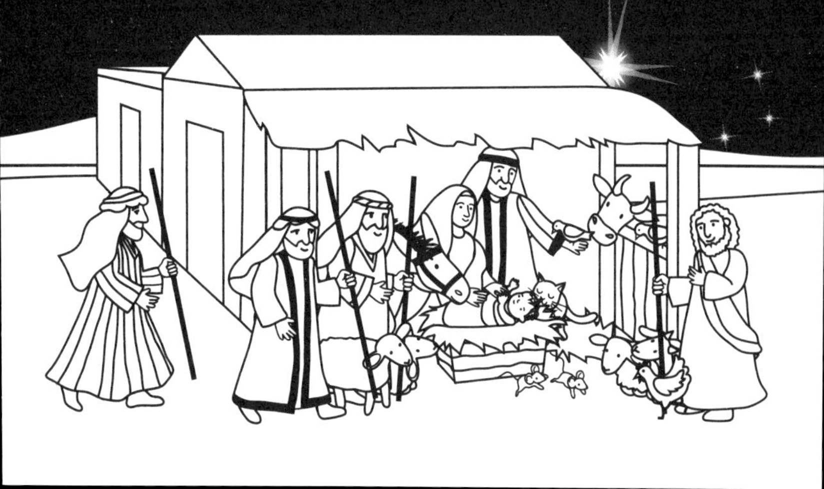

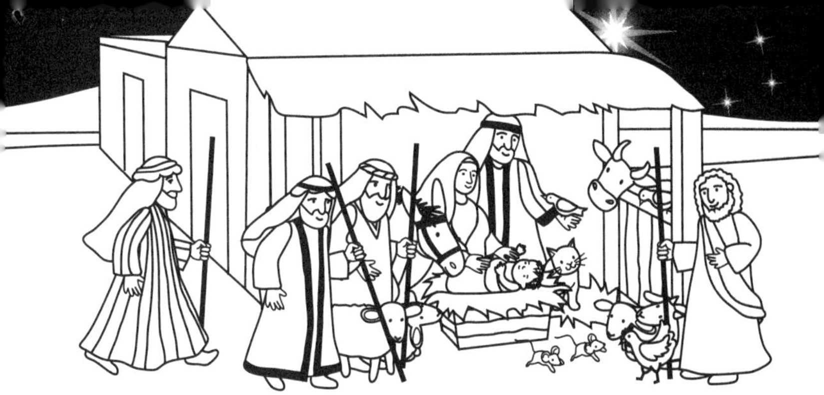

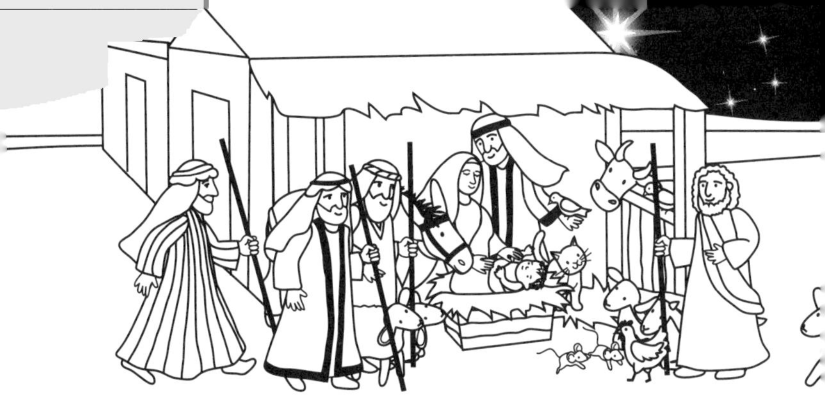

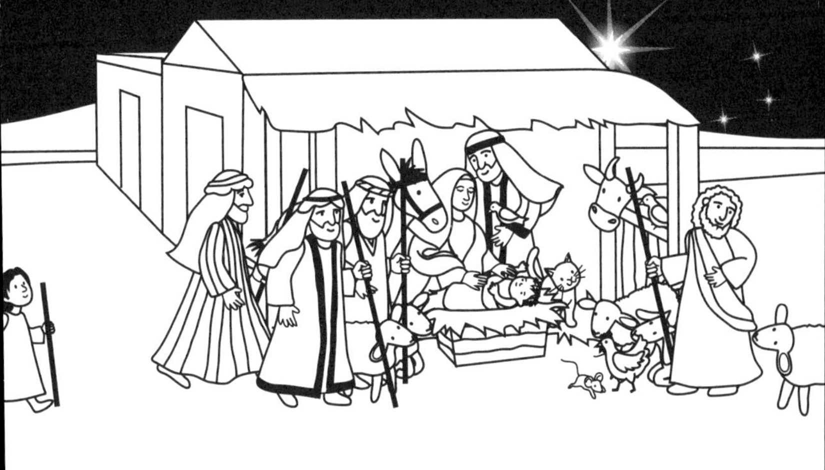

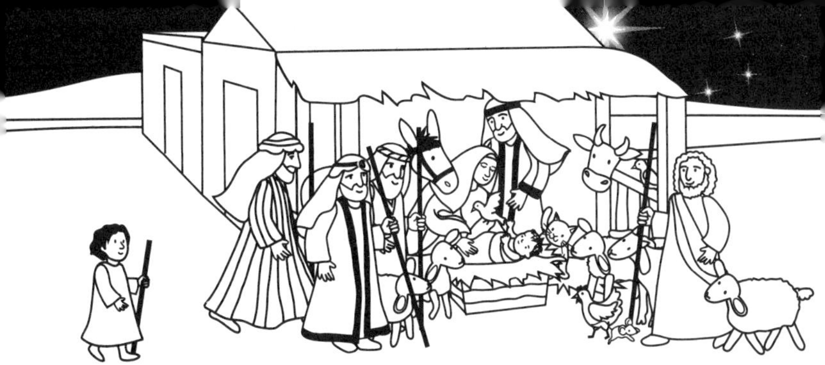

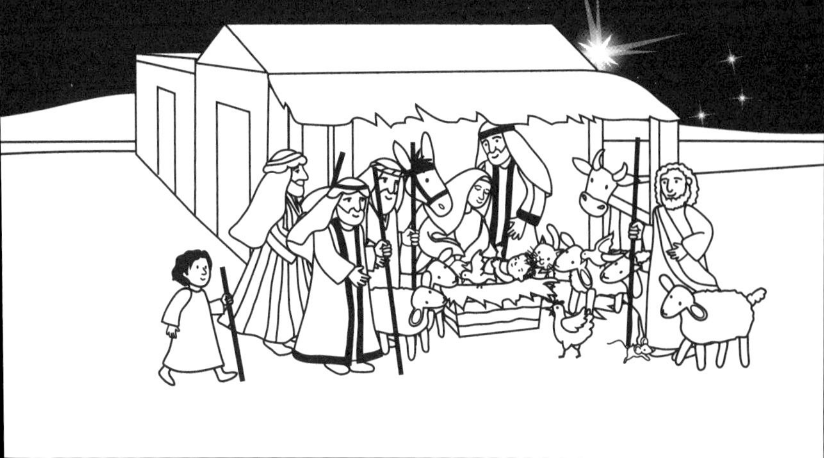

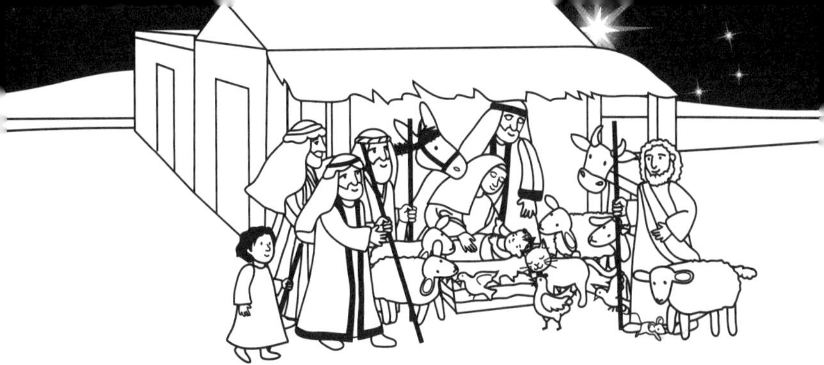

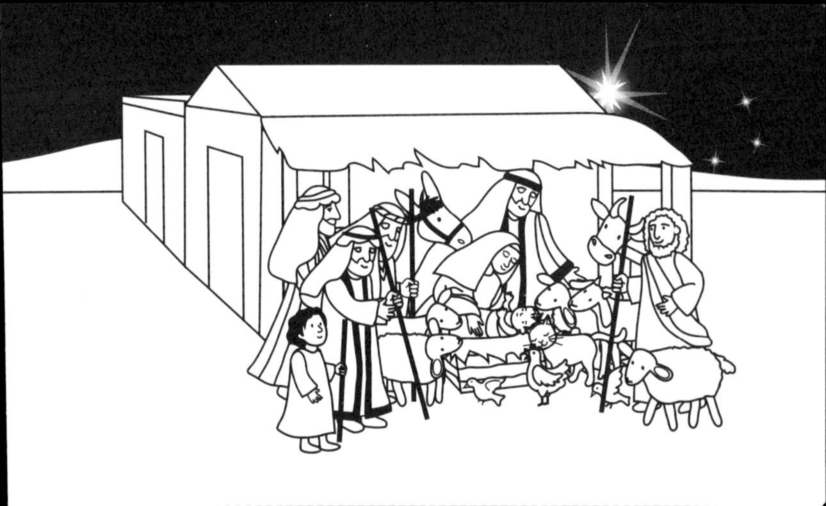

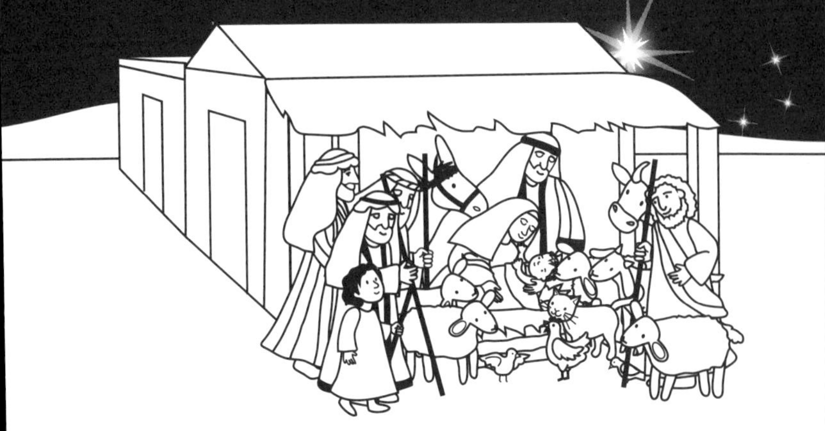

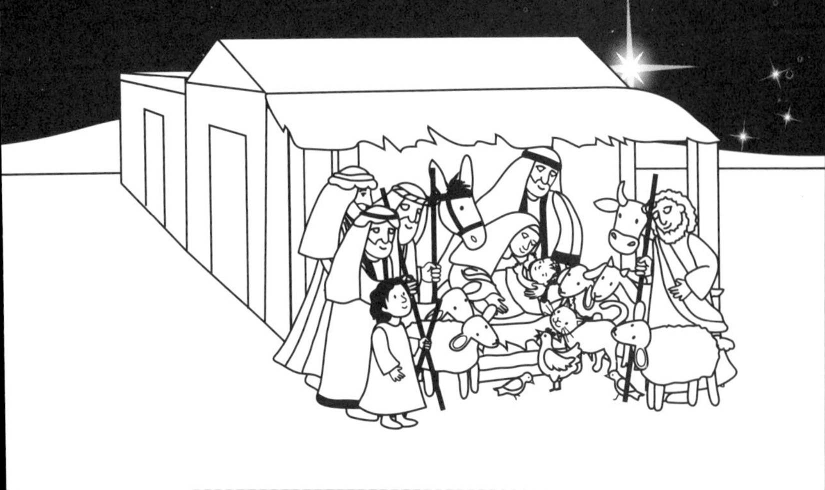

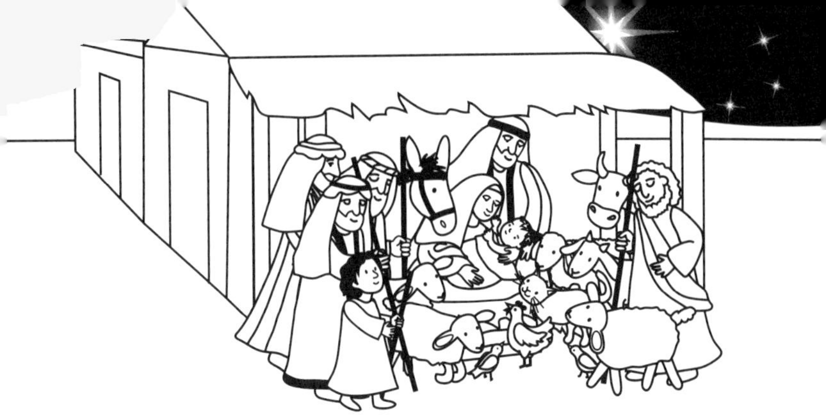

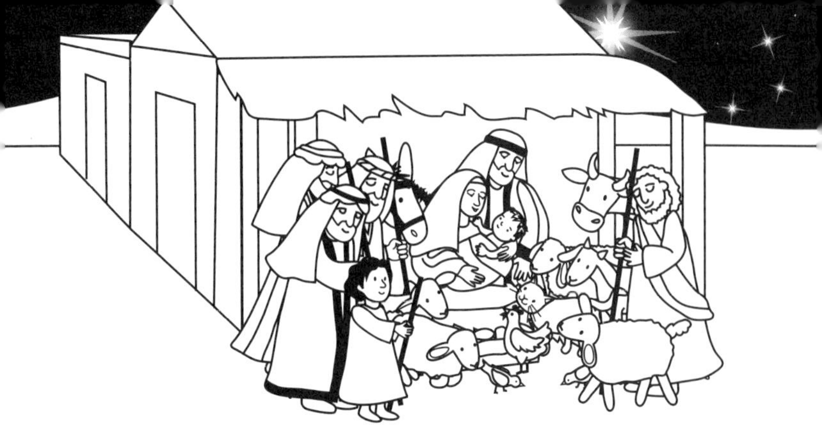

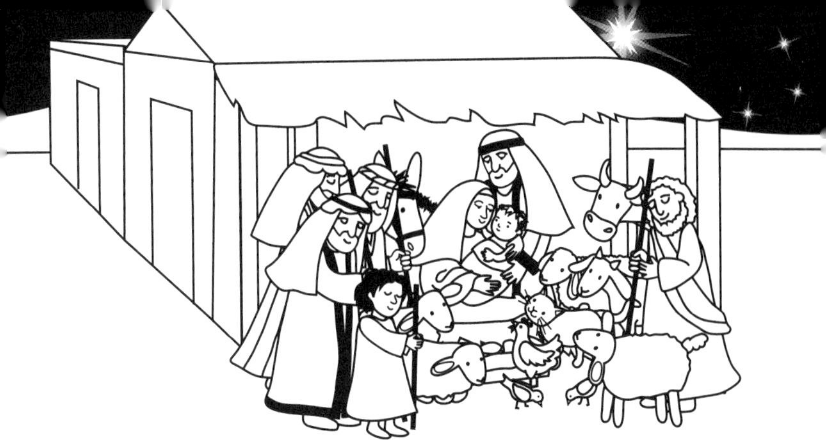

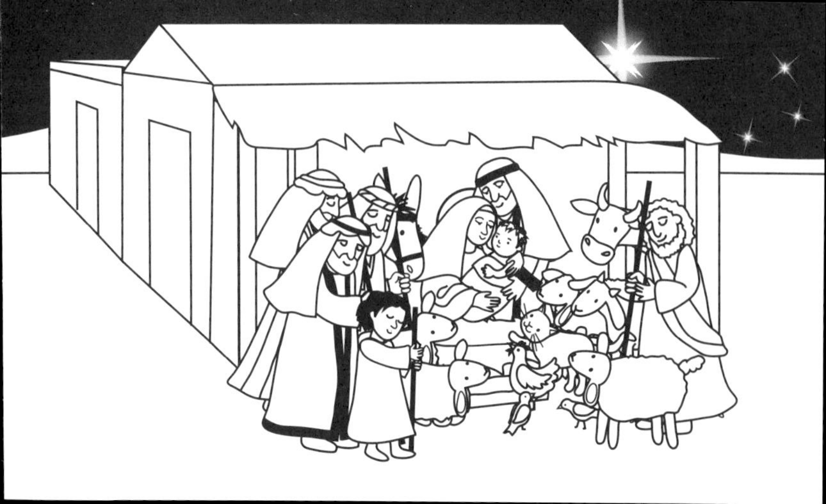

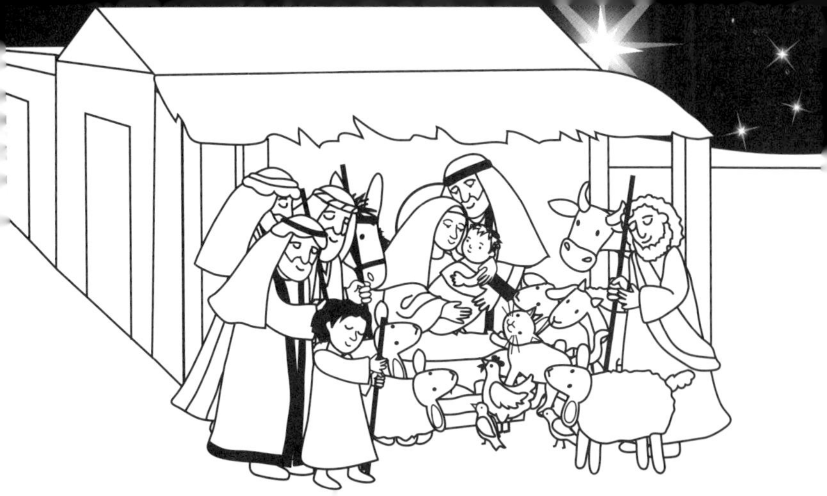

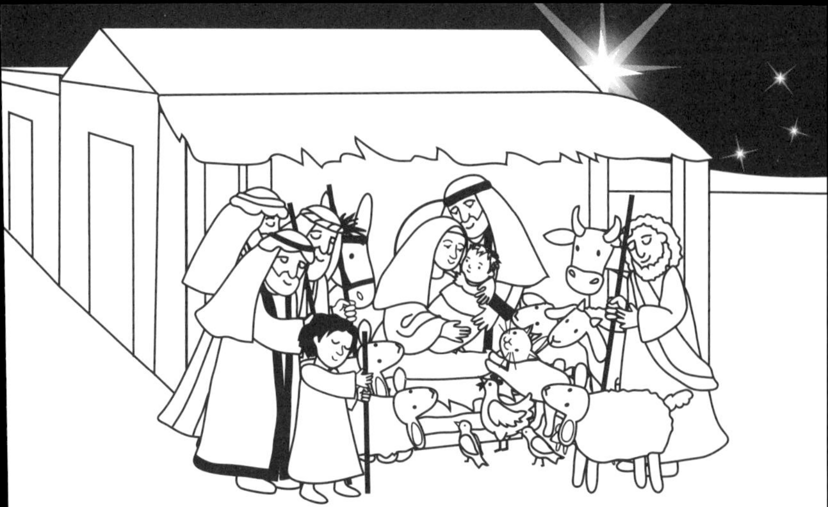

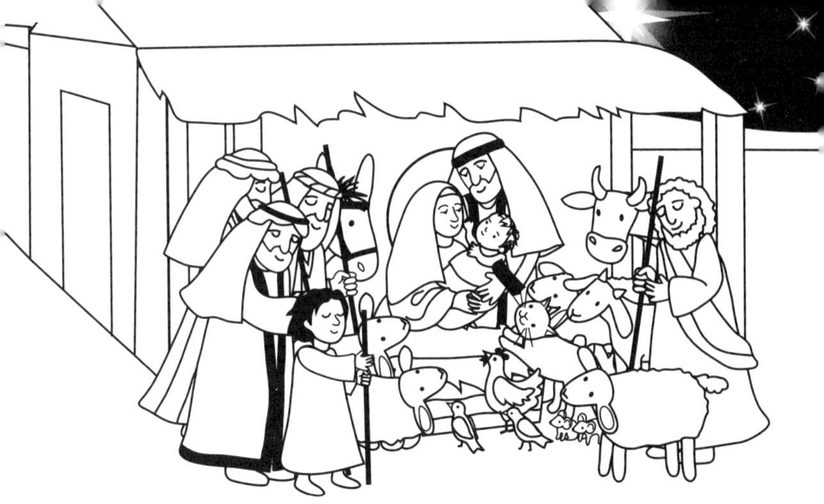

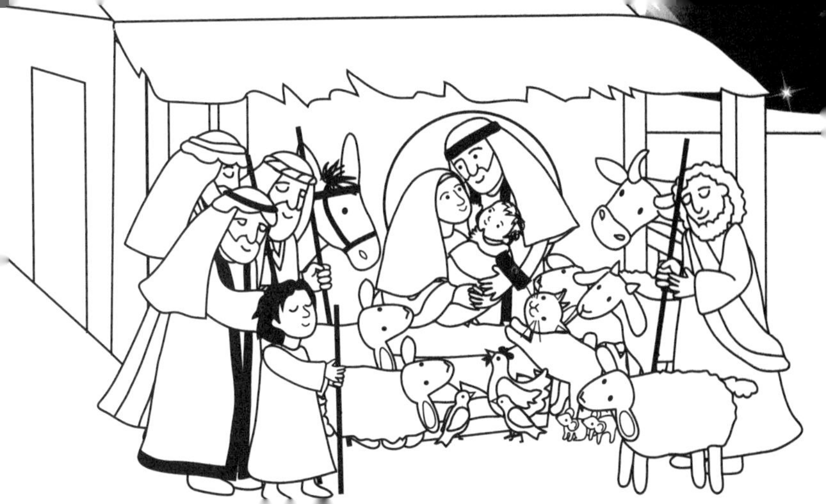

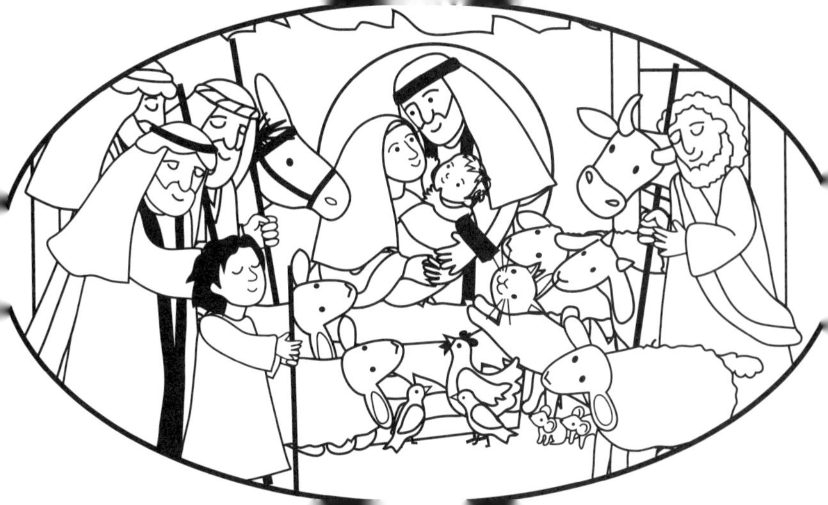

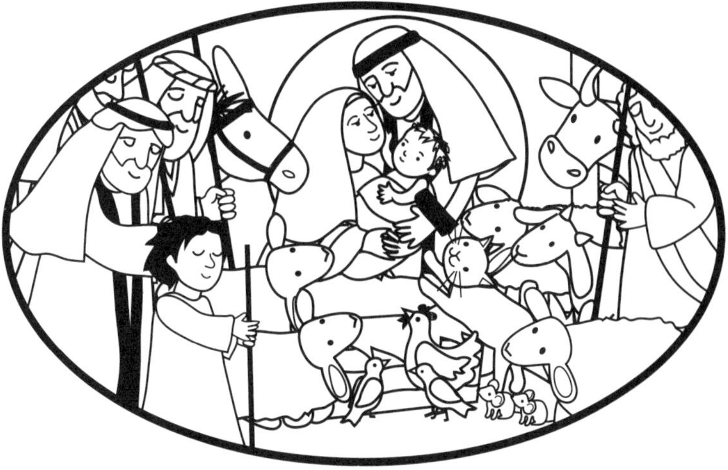

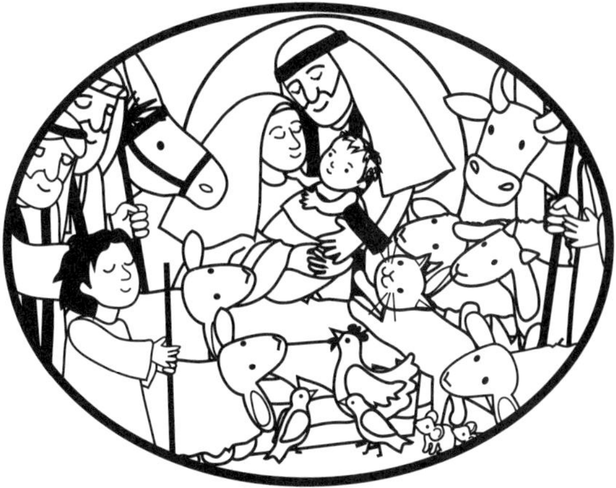

ZONDERKIDZ

Baby Jesus Is Born
Copyright © 2012 by Zondervan
Illustrations © 2012 by Linda Clearwater

Requests for information should be addressed to:

Zonderkidz, 5300 Patterson Ave. S.E., Grand Rapids, Michigan 49530

ISBN 978-0-310-72690-6

All rights reserved. No part of this publication may be reproduced, stored in a retrieval system, or transmitted in any form or by any means—electronic, mechanical, photocopy, recording, or any other—except for brief quotations in printed reviews, without the prior permission of the publisher.

Zonderkidz is a trademark of Zondervan.

Editor: Kim Childress
Design & art direction: Kris Nelson

Printed in China

12 13 14 15 16 / LPC / 22 21 20 19 18 17 16 15 14 13 12 11 10 9 8 7 6 5 4 3 2 1